GRIEVING FOR MY BABY

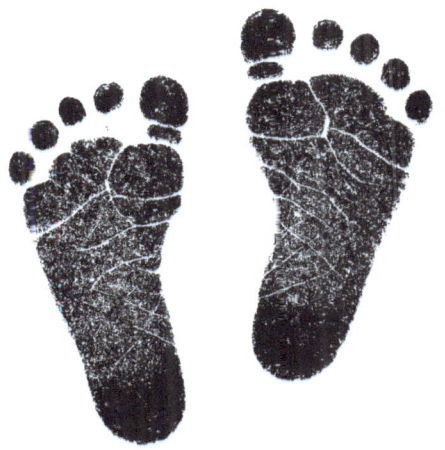

Written & compiled by

PATRICIA M LYONS

Copyright © 2025
First Published in Australia in 2025
By Morpheus Publishing
Geelong Victoria 3216
www.morpheuspublishing.com.au

All rights reserved. No part of this publication may be reproduced, stored in a retrieval system, or transmitted in any form or by any means, electronic, mechanical, photocopying, recording or otherwise, without the prior written permission of the publisher or author.

Paperback ISBN: 978-1-7641639-1-0
Author: **Patricia Lyons**
Editor: Justine Martin
Cover Graphics: Mylen Carascal

A catalogue record for this book is available from the National Library of Australia.

DISCLAIMER
The information contained in this book is for general informational purposes only. The author and publisher are not offering any medical, legal or professional advice. While every effort has been made to ensure the accuracy and completeness of the information provided, the author and publisher assume no responsibility for errors or omissions or any outcomes or consequences resulting from using this book's content.

COPYRIGHT
All original material in this book is the sole property of the author and Morpheus Publishing.

DISTRIBUTION
This book is distributed by Morpheus Publishing and is available through authorised distributors, booksellers, Morpheus Publishing website.

COPYRIGHT PERMISSIONS
For copyright permissions or any other inquiries, please contact:

PUBLISHER: Morpheus Publishing
www.morpheuspublishing.com.au | hello@morpheuspublising.com.au | +61403 564 942

AUTHOR: Patricia Lyons
https://www.morpheuspublishing.com.au/authors/patricia-lyons

A huge thank you to
my friend and consultant,
Ann-Maree Imrie.

Dedicated to
Cameron and Mackellar.
You would have loved your big brother!

TABLE OF CONTENTS

Foreword vii

Introduction 1

Part One: Levi's Farewell 3

Part Two: The Realisation Sets In 9

Part Three: Coming To Terms, But Still Hurting 17

Part Four: Questions and Anger – Do They Ever Stop? ... 29

Part Five: Trying to Escape Reality 35

Part Six: Feelings 43

Part Seven: Feels Like I'm Going Backwards,
Trying to Look Forward 51

Part Eight: Special Events – They Don't Feel So Special
Anymore 65

25 Years On 77

FOREWORD

I met Patricia in the late summer of 2003. We became firm, forever friends. She was tall, graceful, a former dancer. She was organised, funny, passionate, oh so very organised; something I most certainly am not. You knew instantly with Patricia that here was a woman who treasures her relationships. Once Patricia is your friend, you know she's a friend for life.

Patricia carried within her a devastating story—the death of her firstborn, Levi. People who have experienced such an unspeakable loss walk through the world differently. Everything in their lives is called into question. As they pass through the fire, the banal and unimportant fall away, and they are left with a vulnerability and clarity of vision that others cannot possibly understand. They know the worst; they've experienced it. They live it every day.

Patricia was no exception. What was different about her, though, was her willingness to speak to me about Levi as if he were still in her arms. Not in a worrying way, but with peace, love and joy, focused on the gifts he had brought her in his very short life. A totally natural expression of a mother's love for her child. So many people are afraid of death.

They are afraid of the dying, and they are afraid of the living who remain. They don't speak about death, they don't acknowledge the person who has died, nor the ongoing weight that the bereaved will carry forever.

On Mother's Day that year, a few months after we met, Patricia and I were sitting together in church. The mothers were being celebrated. Patricia painfully sat in the place of being a mother but not being a mother. She had no child to give her chocolates like all the other mothers in the room. Most people didn't know she was a mother, but I did. I whispered to her that she is a mum and made sure she was given chocolates. Patricia didn't stop being a mother because her son had died. She is mum to three children, not just the two who have grown into young adults. Levi's birthday is honoured just as her living children's birthdays are.

In order to fully know her as my friend, Patricia knew I needed to know all of her, and that included knowing Levi, who is, after all, a part of her. She told me how he lived, and she also told me how he died. She talked to me about the beginning of her journey of healing. She gave me a book of poetry she had written, a book where her overwhelming grief, the physical ache in her heart, her tears and her love poured out onto the page. This book is a book of healing for herself. But such is the soul of Patricia— her kindness and her empathy—that she wanted to help others who had experienced the grief that she had. Her hope was that, through her poetry and her vulnerability, others would feel heard and held. Grief never ends, nor should it. Grief is an expression of love, and as with love, grief simply shape-shifts with time.

There is a picture of Levi hanging on the wall in Patricia's house. Her husband and her children know Levi well, even though they have never met. He is part of their family. He is loved. He is carried in all of their hearts.

My favourite poem is by e.e. cummings. It feels apt to share it here in the foreword of a book of poetry written by a woman who knows:

i carry your heart with me (i carry it in
 my heart) i am never without it (anywhere
 i go you go, my dear; and whatever is done
 by only me is your doing, my darling) i fear
 no fate (for you are my fate, my sweet) i want
 no world (for beautiful you are my world, my true)
 and it's you are whatever a moon has always meant
 and whatever a sun will always sing is you

here is the deepest secret nobody knows
 (here is the root of the root and the bud of the bud
 and the sky of the sky of a tree called life; which grows
 higher than soul can hope or mind can hide)
 and this is the wonder that's keeping the stars apart
 i carry your heart (i carry it in my heart)

— **Angharad Candlin**
July 2025

INTRODUCTION

This book of poems and letters was written after my little baby boy, Levi Maurice, died suddenly of Pneumococcal Pneumonia, at fourteen and a half months of age. Pneumococcal Pneumonia is a bacterial infection of the lungs that often displays no symptoms and can very quickly become fatal.

I would especially like to thank my family, all my church family at Telopea Church of Christ (then) and City Central Church (now), the mothers from Ermington Spurway Playgroup, friends, and family & friends overseas.

Thank you for all your overwhelming support and encouragement throughout my life. I never would have made it this far without the strength and gifts God has given me, and all these wonderful people.

Levi was a very happy, content and easy-going little boy. We did everything together. He was my best friend and my world. I miss him terribly; may he rest in peace with the Lord.

        Patricia M Lyons (nee: Rasker)

PART ONE

LEVI'S FAREWELL

The following poems were written
specifically for the funeral, to bid farewell
to a very special little boy.

God's beautiful little creation
Has been taken back;
Why, we'll never know.

He wanted this one for himself,
Although we all loved him so.

Patricia Rasker - 13/9/99

*Written on the memorial cards given to family
and friends at his funeral.*

WITH LOVE FROM MAMA

My little munchkin man
You are so sweet;
With your cute little laugh,
And your stumpy little feet.

Your smile and your love,
I will never forget;
Having you bless my life,
I can't ever regret.

Now I leave you in God's hands.
And with my mother there too;
Sleep well, my baby boy(and never forget...)
Your mama loves you.

Patricia Rasker - 13/9/99

The last two lines are what I used to say to Levi, as I put him down in his cot to sleep each night.

A LETTER FROM OPA AND OMA

Dear Levi,

Opa and Oma are a little sad today. But we know you are on your way to a beautiful land. Opa had planned to do so many things with you!

- Rumble on the floor.
- Kick a ball in the park.
- Teach you to mow my lawn.

But other things were planned for you.

So goodbye, little boy,

Till we meet again.

Stuart Rasker – Sept 1999

I am of Dutch descent, and Opa and Oma are grandfather and grandmother in Dutch.

GOODBYE

Once you've left, please don't forget,
I'll always love you so.
Mem'ries of you will never fade,
As I won't let them go.

You've become a special part of me,
That no one else will see;
As this is a special part,
That is only known to me.

God held out his hand to take you now,
Though why, I cannot understand.
I know you'll be cared for and are at peace,
In a far more beautiful land.

But now the time has come,
And I can't help but to cry.
Before you go, just one last thing,
I love you, Levi. Goodbye.

Patricia Rasker – 13/9/99

This poem was read out by my brother Richard Rasker, before Levi's tiny casket disappeared from view to Gina Jeffrey's song, "Distant Star".

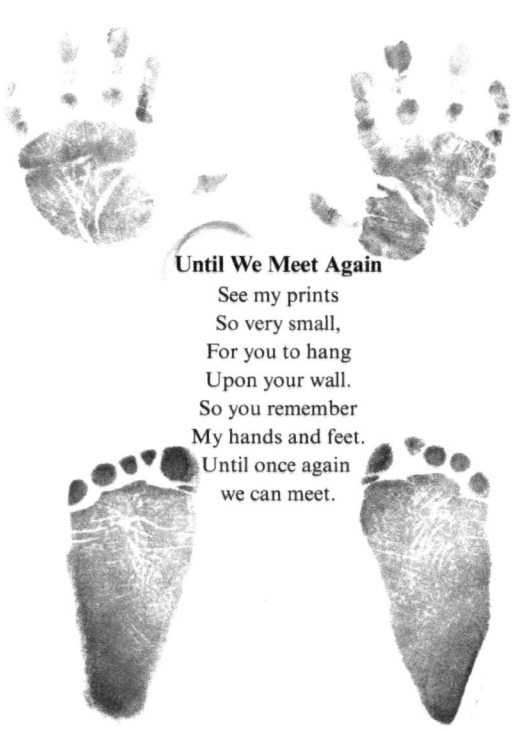

Until We Meet Again
See my prints
So very small,
For you to hang
Upon your wall.
So you remember
My hands and feet.
Until once again
we can meet.

Patricia Rasker - Sept 1999

These are a copy of the hand & foot prints that I received from Westmead Forensic Medicine, after Levi's autopsy. I was also given a lock of his hair.

PART TWO

THE REALISATION SETS IN

A CHILD LOANED

"I'll lend you for a little time,
a child of mine." He said.
"For you to love while he lives,
and mourn for when he's dead.
It may be one or two years,
or twenty-two or three;
But will you till I call him back,
Take care of him for me?
He'll bring his charms to gladden you,
And should his stay be brief,
You'll have his loving memories,
as solace for your grief."

"I cannot promise he will stay,
since all from Earth return,
But there are lessons taught down there,
I want this child to learn.
I've searched this wide world over,
In my search for teachers' true,
And from the crowds that throng life's lanes,
I have selected you.
Now will you give him all your love,
Nor think the labour vain;
Nor hate me when I come to call,
And take him back again."

continued…

> I fancied that I heard them say,
> "Dear Lord, Thy will be done.
> For all the joy thy child shall bring,
> The risk of grief we'll run.
> We'll shelter him with tenderness,
> We'll love him while we may.
> And for the happiness we've known,
> forever grateful, stay.
> But should the angels call for him,
> Much sooner than we'd planned,
> We'll brave the bitter grief that comes,
> and try to understand."

Edgar A Guest
1881 – 1959

This poem was given to me by my very special friend and my spiritual mentor at the time, Vicki Payne (also a bereaved parent), at a memorial service held for Levi, at Telopea Church of Christ, on 23/9/99. I was, after reading this poem, even more thankful for the time that I had with Levi, and very proud that God had chosen me to be his mum, and love him.

EMPTY AND HOLLOW

Empty and hollow, that's how I feel;
Like a tube that's made of cold, hard steel.
My heart feels numb and I don't think I can cry.
I'm all cried out I feel, and when I'm blue,
All that comes is a heavy sigh.

It's a strange feeling, one I've never had;
Though I loved my mum, when she left,
I still wasn't this sad.

The death of your child, nothing can compare;
The feeling's unique, nothing you can share.
Empty and hollow, the words to describe,
The confusion, the hurt and the pain inside.

Patricia Rasker - 30/9/99

WHAT I'D GIVE

The house is starting to look bare.
All the toys have gone.
How I'd give anything right now to see you playing,
As I listen to Gina, sing your song.

I've never felt so empty and lonely,
Though I've been and lived alone before.
Sometimes I still find it hard to believe and I expect,
To see you crawling through the door.

Just to hear your laugh and to watch you play,
I'd give everything on this earth.
I will always remember the fun we've had together,
Starting way back from your birth.

All that I am, and all that I have,
I'd give up to be with you now.
If only I could, you know that I would;
If only I knew how.

I still don't know why you left.
At such a very young age.
So sweet, so innocent, and so vulnerable too,
Sometimes it fills me with so much rage.

But my baby boy, you know what I'd give,
And it's what I'd give most of;
If I could hold you now, just one more time,
I'd give you all my love.

Patricia Rasker – 30/9/99

MIND, HEART AND SOUL

Out of sight, out of mind;
No, that's definitely not true for me.
You'll always be in my mind, heart and soul;
Locked in my memory.
God loaned you to me, to take care of you,
And at that, I did the best I could.
Now the angels came to take you back;
I knew eventually they would.

I just thought I'd go first,
And you'd be burying me.
I'm happy you've been saved from that pain,
Though, nor did I want it for myself.
But the grief and pain are worth it now,
For the times that we did share.
Even if it was only a very short time,
I'm so glad that you were there.
I wouldn't do it differently,
If I could do life over again.
You'll always be in my mind, heart and soul,
And be my little man.

Patricia Rasker – 1/10/99

I took Levi to playgroup every Tuesday,
and so we had the hard task of explaining his
death to his friends there.
The other mothers at playgroup,
came up with this beautiful little poem,
which they put in the newsletter so Levi's friends
could say goodbye to him.
Thank you girls, this really touched me,
more than you can imagine.

Bye-bye Levi, from your friends at
Ermington Spurway Playgroup.

This is a poem to say goodbye,
To our little friend, his name, Levi.
On playgroup day we miss your smile,
Your face, your laugh, your cheeky style.
We see your mum, and know she is sad,
So together we remember the good times had.
Our mums have said to pick a star,
So we will always know just where you are.

PART THREE

COMING TO TERMS, BUT STILL HURTING

LEVI

L is for love. The love that I feel;
That's never lost or gone.
E is for energy. There was so much of that;
Like the sun, you really shone.
V is for vivacious. You were so alive;
So happy and content.
I is for individual. You were and are unique;
No doubt about it, heaven-sent.

But to me, **L E V I** means so much
more than just these words;
He means my little boy and a part of me,
That's never lost and will never die;
We'll be together again Levi, you'll see.

Patricia Rasker – 1/10/99

I KNOW I'LL BE OK

Up till now, I always had too little time;
Just wanted five minutes' rest.
Now, there is nothing but time –
That's all I have.
I still wake so early, so the days are long;
And sometimes it's like being concussed,
As I plod through the day with nothingness.

The times when I'm with friends,
And I'm having a good time, I feel.
Like I'm standing outside my body watching.
I'm just watching myself laugh.
I think, how can I be enjoying myself?
When a part of me just died.

But I found you do;
You do cope and get on.
I was so confused, and still am a bit;
It's hard to comprehend the feelings.
I know all this is normal and expected;
The more I read and talk to friends,
I know I'll be ok.

Patricia Rasker – 1/10/99

I MISS YOU SO MUCH

It's been a while since I've written anything,
I haven't known what to write.
Tomorrow is one month to the day,
Since you left and went towards the light.

I miss you so much; my heart cries out.
For you to know I care.
Though life goes on, and jobs get done,
I miss that you're not there.

Levi, sweetheart, come back to me.
I say it as though you could do it with ease;
But that's all I think about all day long,
And at night in my dreams.

I miss you so much, my heart cries out;
You've got to know it's true.
I'm sad and I'm lonely and life's so incomplete,
Without the wonderful joy that is you.

Patricia Rasker – 12/10/99

A LETTER FROM HEAVEN

I was so young and couldn't say
The things I wanted to;
Of how you cared, and how we shared
My life enriched by you.
You're always my eternal mum.
Though time keeps us apart.
The bonds remain, we'll always be,
Held in each other's hearts.

I would have liked to say, "I love you",
All those nights and days;
We were so close, you know I did,
But in my little ways.
I loved to give you my big smile.
You kept me so content.
There never was a better mum;
To me, you're heaven-sent.

I am so pleased you found our Lord,
Before my time to leave.
I'm with Him now, such joy is mine,
But sadly, you must grieve.
Don't search for answers you'll not find;
Instead, let go, release.
Just thank the Lord for moments shared,
And you will find your peace.

I wait to hold you in my arms
The way that you held me.
A love restored, to serve our Lord,
Throughout eternity.

I love you Mum, Levi.

Anon.

This was written especially for me by a close friend of mine from my church, who wishes to remain anonymous. God Bless!

BEAUTIFUL BOY

Beautiful boy, you'll always be
The twinkle in my eye.
You'll always be my guiding light,
The brightest star in my night-time sky.

Beautiful boy, I still show you off,
To everyone I meet.
I tell them of the fun we had,
And how you're so happy and so sweet.

Beautiful boy, I often cry,
I think I always will.
This isn't something that can be fixed,
With an operation or a pill.

Beautiful boy, I see your friends.
The ones you never got to know.
They're walking and some talking now.
I miss that I'll never see you grow.

How I would have loved to see you toddle;
To hear you say "mama", what a joy.
But I guess that just wasn't to be,
Though you'll always be my beautiful boy.

Patricia Rasker – 12/10/99

REMINDERS

Everything's all packed up,
even your bed has gone.
It's all in storage,
or being used by friends or family.
It's all so final now.

I've kept a few things as reminders,
the things I can't let go.
The things that scream out your name;
When I need it most.

I can't believe how quiet it is,
how empty this house is now.
When it used to be so full of life;
And now it's just me.

Your smile stares down at me from
the pictures on the wall.
You're all around this house and everywhere.
But mainly in my heart.

Patricia Rasker - 12/10/99

SO I . . .

So many things I'd like to have taught you;
So much I'd like to have seen you do.
I sit outside, watching the kids play;
I think of you, and all the things I'd like to say.

So little time together here on this earth;
So many memories for what it's worth.
I still can't believe that you're not here.
I can't help, as I remember, but to shed a tear.

So my baby boy, my precious little son;
So munchkin man, my only one.
I will keep you forever locked in my heart;
I know a bond like ours will never part.

So I shall never forget you,
Nor the Lord's promise and love;
So I know that I will see you again,
In heaven, up above.

Patricia Rasker – 13/10/99

LEVI, I'M SCARED

Levi, I'm scared; Of what, I'm not too sure.
Of life without you, I guess.
Everything was going so right,
And now it seems like a mess.

I'm scared of what's going to happen;
It's my life without you, I fear.
Scared that one day I won't,
Won't be shedding this tear.

Levi, I'm scared; Of everything, but mainly;
That one day I'll forget your birthday or anniversary.
Because I may meet someone in the future,
And I'll be so happy I'll forget, and it's scary.

I know in my head that I will never forget;
But I can't help but feel scared in my heart that I could.
I'd never want to forget the joy that was you,
And I doubt that I ever would.

Levi, I'm scared; of changes that happen.
And that you're not here to see and share,
I'll never forget you, no matter what,
But what if... Levi, I'm scared

Patricia Rasker – 13/10/99

IT NEVER OCCURRED TO ME

I miss you so much, I'm hurting.
I'm sad and I'm angry –

all at the same time;
But most of all, I'm lonely.

Why did you go, why now?
When everything was going so good.
You left me all alone;

It never occurred to me you would.

Patricia Rasker – 13/10/99

GOODBYE (NO 2)

Now you've left, please don't forget,
I'll always miss you so.
You'll forever be locked in my heart,
This you already know.

You'll eternally be my baby boy,
Though I'll never see you grow.
We'll be together one day again.
How I long for that day so.

But will you excuse me if I don't run,
Straight to your side right now?
Keep watch over me from up there,
And I shall go on somehow.

So now the time has come, for life to go on,
For those of us not up there in the sky.
I will always love and remember you,
Be a good boy, my baby, goodbye.

Patricia Rasker – 13/10/99

PART FOUR

QUESTIONS AND ANGER – DO THEY EVER STOP?

HOW COME ME?

How come this happened to me?
What did I do wrong?
I did the best I knew how,
But then you left.

I tried to be the best for you;
The best mum in the world.
Then you went to see God,
And never came back.

How come it doesn't happen to others;
Those who neglect their children;
The mothers who don't care anyway?
How come me?

Patricia Rasker – 14/10/99

ANGRY AT LOVE

I'm so angry at you;
Why did you leave me now?
I'm so mad and irate;
Something went wrong somehow.

I'm so angry at love;
Why does it hurt right through?
I'm so confused because,
I'm angry, but I love you.

```
Patricia Rasker - 14/10/99
```

WITHOUT YOU

I'm bored;
Bored with loneliness;
Bored without you.

I'm lonely;
Lonely with just me;
Lonely without you.

I'm sick;
Sick of being alone;
Sick of being without you.

I miss you;
I don't like life,
Without you.

Patricia Rasker – 15/10/99

AND GOD SAID

I said, "God, I hurt."
And God said, "I know."
I said, "God, I cry a lot." And God said,
"That is why I gave you tears."
I said, "God, I am so depressed." And God said,
"That is why I gave you sunshine."
I said, "God, life is so hard." And God said,
"That is why I gave you loved ones."
I said, "God, my loved one died."
And God said, "So did mine."
I said, "God, it is such a loss." And God said,
"I saw mine nailed to a cross."
I said, "God, but your loved one lives."
And God said, "So does yours."
I said, "God, where are they now?" And God said,
"Mine is on my right,
and yours is in the light."
I said, "God, it hurts."
And God said, "I know."

Author Unknown.

This poem was posted at the Oklahoma City bombing site, USA by KC & Myke Kuzmic. I received it in the mail from a good friend at Church who, at the time, I didn't know. It touched me deeply, and brought me out of a very angry state.

PART FIVE

TRYING TO ESCAPE REALITY

I went by train to Melbourne to see friends there. It is a trip that Levi and I did together just six months earlier (almost to the day) - the pain doesn't change. It was just as bad, away from my usual environment. It follows you —no matter where you go.

A BREAK

I'll go for a break, and see some friends; that's a good idea, I thought.

Friends all said to go; it's a good idea, and that I ought to.

But travelling now, on the train, all by myself, I'm blue;

Thinking of the time we did this trip; constantly thinking of you.

I think once I get there, I'll have some fun; I'll be with friends, I should.

It still would be so nice to have you with me; oh, how I wish I could.

Reality doesn't take a break, and still, you're not here with me.

Only every other daydream; each one a wonderful fantasy.

The best one being that this is all a dream, and I wake up nice and warm.

You're waiting for me at the other end, as I step down on the platform.

But alas, reality hits, and it's gone cold again.

I know you're waiting for me somewhere else,

but when I'll see you, I don't know when.

So I'll take this break, and see some friends, surely it can't hurt.

When I return, in two weeks' time, I've got to get back to work.

But travelling now, on the train, all by myself, I realise,

You're watching, helping me get through all this, from up there in the skies.

Thank you baby, for the dreams of you, whether I'm asleep or awake.

And thank you Jesus for helping me to go on, and for giving me the strength to take a break.

Patricia Rasker – 17/10/99

GOD'S KISS

The sun is setting in the western sky;
I ponder just how fast time can fly.
Not so long ago, you were showing me your charms,
And now you're up there, in God's arms.

His arms are big and they can carry you,
Plus, everyone else that is up there too.
God's loving and tender, and He'll take care,
While you're in heaven, somewhere up there.

At the same time, He's watching my heart bleed;
Strengthening me, when I need.
God's so big He can do all this;
Even sends us both to bed with a goodnight kiss.

Patricia Rasker - 17/10/99

Levi baby, come and play
On the train with me today.

Levi baby, I miss you so,
Why, oh why did you have to go?

Patricia Rasker - 17/10/99

Sweetheart, will you forgive me
For being so content and lively?
I am still young and have a life to live
With so much love to give.

You'll always be my baby boy.
No matter who else may bring me joy.
Forgive me that I don't rush to your side;
Instead, look down, and guide me with pride.

Patricia Rasker - 22/10/99

LIFE

On the way home, after having a break,
I'm thinking of life without you.
Thinking of how my life's changing
And all the things I need to do.
I really wish you hadn't gone,
We could've had such a really good life.
Me teaching you right from wrong,
You getting up to mischief and strife.

But alas, I'm heading back home, to start a new life,
A life now on my own.
I miss you so much and the things you do.
It feels like you're all I've ever known.
I have worked before, as I am about to again;
It feels different this time somehow.
I was so prepared to give you my all;
However, you don't need it up there, right now.

So, I'll go to work and plod through life;
To make you proud, I have to try.
Though I'll have my quiet time to remember you,
And take my time to cry.

Patricia Rasker – 30/10/99

I WANT YOU BACK

I'm still angry; at who, I don't know.
At you, at God; whoever made you go.
The loneliness, the boredom; they're still there.
I'm all alone; though I know people care.
But it's not the same; it's not you.
I know they mean well, with the things they do.
It eases the pain, though I still feel I'm going to crack,
'Cause the thing they can't do, is to bring you back.

```
Patricia Rasker - 30/10/99
```

PART SIX
FEELINGS

IT'S ALL ABOUT ME

We had such a good thing going
I had a really great life for us planned
I had everything I always wanted
My very own precious little child, you.

I did everything for you, Levi
As much as we could, we did together
My life was all about you
And now it's gone, you're gone.

So what am I supposed to do now
I'm not used to living for me
Everything I do now is for myself
And that just doesn't feel right.

I want you back
I want to do things for you again
I don't want to start over
I hate it that now, it's all about me.

Patricia Rasker – 3/11/99

MUM

It's your turn Mum, to hold the baby;
We've all had a go.
I know you've waited for this,
To cuddle him too;
You've longed to kiss him, I know.

Now he's with you, in God's kingdom;
In heaven up above.
Care for him, Mum, like you cared for me;
And give him all your love.

I'll join you both one day,
I hope not too soon, though.
It'll be Mum, me and baby.
For now, mum, take care.
And do me this favour;
Give him a kiss from me.

Patricia Rasker – 9/11/99

When I was 21, my mother passed away from a rare form of Leukemia. It's nice to know that Levi is not only with God, but also with his grandmother.

DOING TIME

A life sentence
Is what it feels like
Since the loss of you.

What once was our family home
Has now become
My cell of mem'ries of you.

My world was torn apart;
A knife cut into my heart.
Hurting right through;
Doing time in pain for you.

Patricia Rasker – 14/11/99

BEST FRIEND

Not only were you my baby,
Not only my little boy;
You were more than just my son,
More than just a bundle of joy.

You were all things
From start to end;
But on top of these things,
You were my **best friend**.

Patricia Rasker – 14/11/99

I LAID YOUR ASHES DOWN TO REST TODAY

I laid your ashes down to rest today,
And said a little prayer.
I asked that they be blessed and kept safe
Oma & Opa too, were there.

I laid your ashes down to rest today,
Though I didn't want to part.
Maybe if I held on tight enough, I thought
You'd come back, outside my heart.

Levi baby, I miss you lots.
You know it's true, I pray.
Another chapter of you has now closed;
I laid your ashes down to rest today.

Patricia Rasker - 15/11/99

CAR 980

I know you did all you could
I know that you tried
I know you felt my pain
I saw it when you cried.

You were quick to come to my aid
You were quick to take control
You did well to try and comfort me
As I was losing part of my soul.

Thank you for your efforts
Thanks for all that you tried to do
I don't know quite what to say
I just want to say **thank you**.

Patricia Rasker – 21/2/00

I would like to take this opportunity to thank Car 980 from the New South Wales Ambulance Service and the staff at Westmead Children's Hospital, Sydney, for all their efforts on the morning that Levi passed away. I know that they all did everything they could, and I appreciate their work, compassion and understanding.

PART SEVEN

FEELS LIKE I'M GOING BACKWARDS, TRYING TO LOOK FORWARD

A LETTER TO GOD

God, I'm lonely and sad;
I miss my precious son.
There was no one else in my life –
Here on earth, he was the only one.

God, help me;
I'm feeling so down & blue.
I know he is in a beautiful place,
I know that he is with You.

God, but that doesn't help,
The loneliness in my heart;
The emptiness I feel right now
Ever since we had to part.

God, give me strength;
I know in my heart that You do.
Look after my baby boy, dear God,
Until I can be there too.

Patricia Rasker – 23/11/99

I MISS YOU

You were so alive,
So happy, so there.
Anything would happen,
And you didn't seem to care.

You were so easygoing all the time
So bubbly and content.
Nothing seemed to trouble you;
Even just before you went.

But now it's all so quiet.
So empty and so lonely.
I miss your laugh and your smile,
I miss you here with me.

Patricia Rasker - 23/11/99

Last night was a bad night.
I cried myself to sleep again.
There hasn't been a full night's sleep
Not since you left back then.

I cry a lot in my bed
When I'm thinking of you.
Pondering what I have to wake up for.
Thinking there's nothing
To look forward to.

Where I used to go to bed
Looking forward to tomorrow.
Without you now, all I look to
Is another lonely day, full of sorrow.

Patricia Rasker – 23/11/99

BACK TO THE START

It's all coming back;
The restless nights.
The tears and the sadness,
The hurt inside.

It never went away;
It just occasionally eases off.
Opposite to my feelings for you,
My constant, strong love.

I've gone back to how I felt,
The night after you died.
All that I did that night,
Is lay in bed and cried.

I cry so hard and cry so much;
Sometimes I feel like it won't stop.
It hurts so bad, and I feel so alone;
I doubt I'll ever get back on top.

Patricia Rasker - 23/11/99

JOY IS IN THE PAST

Sick of cooking for one.
Cooking used to be fun.
I'd explain just what to do;
Sitting in the highchair,
Learning, was you.

Tired of feeling sad.
Don't like always feeling bad.
Life used to be such a blast;
Now it seems all the joy is in the past.

Patricia Rasker - 23/11/99

DO YOU REMEMBER?

Do you remember my kisses,
My touch, my smile and my love?
Can you recall the fun we had,
And how I made you laugh?

Do you remember the stories I read,
And how you loved them so?
Do you still like to hear them up there,
Since the morning you had to go?

Do you remember the games we played?
Do you remember my voice?
Can you still taste the food that I cooked?
You used to think it was so nice.

Do you remember the baths you took?
You used to love to brush your teeth.
Do you remember the laughs we had drying,
And me tickling your cute, stumpy feet?

Do you remember the morning you left,
That morning in September?
That's one thing I hope you do forget;
Though I will always remember.

Do you hate me for standing by;
You know there was nothing I could do.
All I could do was hold you close,
And tell you how much I loved you.

So, munchkin man, never forget that love;
Carry it always up there, with you.
Because when I close my eyes and think of all this,
I remember it all, I do.

Patricia Rasker – 24/11/99

KEEP THIS TRAIN STEADY

My world was turned upside-down,
Like a train derailed,
Then along came you.
You made it so right and good,
So clear and so true.

For your sake then, and in your name,
I know that I should
Keep this train steady on its track
And keep my life good.

Patricia Rasker – 25/11/99

WHAT CAN I SAY

What can I say; I miss you.
What can I say; I'm lonely.
What can I say; I'm sick of feeling like this.
What can I say; I have nothing more to say.

Patricia Rasker - 29/11/99

TILL I CAN BE UP THERE TOO

God, does it ever end?
Does this bad feeling ever go away?
How about you make it right, and bring him back?
Hey, how about it, what do you say?

I know that you can't do that.
The thing that I want most of all,
Is the one thing that would make me complete again
To see my baby smile, to see him crawl.

Look after him up there,
Till I can be up there too.
Tell him always how I love him and miss him so,
So he'll know me when I come to see You.

Patricia Rasker – 12/12/99

ANGRY

Now I'm confused; Who do I get angry at?
I'm angry at God for letting this happen.
I'm angry at Levi for going.
I'm angry at me for not being able to do anything.
I'm angry at the world for just going on.

Patricia Rasker – 12/12/99

PLEASE DON'T FORGET ME

Will you know me?
You were so young.
I'd like to think you would.
I want to kiss you and hold you tight.
God, tonight, if only I could.

Will you recognise me when I walk in the light?
And I'm heading straight towards you.
Will you run into my arms and give me a smile?
Never forget me, nor my love for you.

Patricia Rasker – 31/12/99

PART EIGHT

SPECIAL EVENTS – THEY DON'T FEEL SO SPECIAL ANYMORE

I'm finding the lead-up to special events tends to be worse than the day itself. Friends rally around on the day itself (for which I am thankful for), but the days and weeks leading up to the actual day can often be just as bad, if not worse.

THE FIRST CHRISTMAS

This will be my first Christmas without you.
And I miss not having you here.
The first of many I have to face without you
And I can't help but shed a tear.
They say time heals all wounds.
But right now I don't believe it's true.
It's times like Christmas when I notice it more.
The empty void in my life that's you.

The mem'ries are still there, so clear.
Of the one Christmas we did share;
But now the festive season's back again
And I wish that you were there.
I'm not feeling all that merry this year.
Not in the mood for all that joy;
I just want one thing for Christmas now.
To be with my baby boy.

Continued…

Christmas is for the kids, they say
But is that only for those who live & breathe?
What about the ones held in God's arms
The ones that belong to you and me.
I know that Santa can't bring me.
The present I so desperately need.
The one thing my heart longs for most of all
Is the thing that would stop it bleed.

Christmas-time cuts me like a knife.
And I'm hurting real bad this year.
It's my first Christmas without you, Levi.
And I know it's ok not to cheer.

Patricia Rasker - 5/11/99

WHAT'S THE POINT

What's the point of Christmas,
Now you're not here with me?
What's the use of hanging balls,
And tinsel on a tree?

I know in my head that Christ was born,
And we need to celebrate;
But in my heart, all I feel,
Is Christmas without you, is not that great.

Patricia Rasker - 24/11/99

A NEW YEAR

A new year - just another year,
The pain will still be the same.
You won't come back at the stroke of midnight.
No matter how much I scream your name.

A new year - a new beginning
In theory, yes it's true.
I'm starting a new chapter of my life.
But it hurts that this one's not with you.

Patricia Rasker – 12/12/99

CHRISTMAS WITHOUT YOU

Levi, I'm hurting;
The pain still seems so new.
Christmas has just made it all so fresh,
Christmas without you.

Tomorrow is three months to the day,
And it's not getting any better.
I can't imagine my family without you.
Celebrating, having Christmas dinner.

I cry each time I think of it.
How it's going to be.
It will all seem so incomplete.
Dad & Joann, Richard & Heather with Rachel…
and just me.

Levi, I'm hurting;
And the pain it cuts right through.
This will be a lonely Christmas, I fear.
Christmas without you.

Patricia Rasker – 12/12/99

NEW YEAR'S EVE

Happy New Year, my little man.
I hope you're being good.
Who will I kiss at midnight?
You know it's you that I wish I could.

I've met someone new to start the new year.
How I wish you could meet, you two.
What do you think, looking down from up there?
I would have loved for him to know you.

So a new year dawns, a chance to start again.
Sweetheart, I wish that you were here.
Midnight will come, and I'll think of you,
And I'll shed a little tear.

Patricia Rasker – 31/12/99

MOTHER'S DAY

Mother's Day has been and gone.
It wasn't that much joy this year.
I don't feel like a real mum, and it's
not quite the same.
Not without you here.

I miss that I won't ever,
Hear you say "Happy Mother's Day Mum",
I'll never get a homemade card.
Or a lovely egg for breakfast,
That's way overdone.

It's the little things on Mother's Day
The presents and the hype won't
make me happy;
All I wanted for Mother's Day
was a cuddle,
From my precious little baby.

Patricia Rasker – 11/6/00

A (NOT SO) HAPPY BIRTHDAY

Happy birthday, special man;
No, we won't sing that song!
Remember how it made you cry,
Though it didn't last that long.
Just think, now you are 2.
What a big, beautiful boy you'd be.
You always were a beautiful boy,
That's locked deep in my memory.

I miss you Levi, more and more
Whether it's your birthday, baby, or not.
But birthdays remind me of
the special things,
that I now have to miss out.

Patricia Rasker – 9/6/00
For Levi's 2nd birthday, 1 July 2000.

A PRAYER FOR YOUR BIRTHDAY (EXTRA KISSES)

Dear God, hold him close.
For today is a special day.
Give him extra kisses from me,
And tell him what I want to say.
Tell him that I love him,
And how I miss him so.
Not just on his birthday,
But each day, as you know.

Wish him a happy birthday from his mum.
Celebrate up in heaven tonight.
Make him feel special on this day,
And make his birthday be a delight.
I know you're taking good care of him,
My big boy, who's 2 today.
Dear God, hold him close by your side,
For today is a special day.

Patricia Rasker - 11/6/00

(For 1 July 2000)

THE PAIN
THAT DOESN'T SHOW

I can't believe it's been a year
Since I've held you close.
How I've coped and made it through,
Only God will ever know.
It seems like only yesterday.
That you were in my arms, so soft;
But yet it feels like an eternity,
That I've been without your love.

Almost a year's gone by;
It's just too unreal.
So many memories to hold on to;
So many feelings to feel.
Baby boy, I miss you more,
Then anyone will <u>ever</u> know.
They don't see the hurt inside,
The pain that doesn't show.

Patricia Rasker – 17/8/00

IT'S SO CLEAR TO ME

Why don't people care?
Why can't they see?
I'm hurting and torn inside;
It's so clear to me.
Friends don't feel;
They can't see
I'm hurting and torn inside;
Yet it's so clear to me.

When I need them,
And they're not there,
I feel so alone;
I feel so scared.
I know it's not fair
To expect them just to know,
But it hurts just the same;
Doesn't the pain show?
It's so clear to me.

Patricia Rasker – 18/8/00

25 YEARS ON

By the grace of God, I have been able to rebuild my life. It took time and a lot of patience and self-care, but I am proof that it is possible. I was a single mother, and Levi was my world. I had given up work, and everything I did was for Levi or to make me a better mum for him.

I have since married Angus Lyons (in 2004) and we have two beautiful children, Cameron and Mackellar. God has blessed me enormously. Of course, it is all so bittersweet, as I love my life now, but I would love it so much more if Levi were in it with me and his new family. He would have adored his younger brother and sister.

Time does heal, and while there are times it certainly won't feel like it, I can assure you that while you won't ever get over losing a child, you can learn to live with the pain. No two people are alike, and everyone has their own way of doing things and their own timing.

Be kind to yourself. Let others help – even if it's just to listen to you waffle on… that's okay!

I was fortunate enough to come to The Lord 2½ months prior to Levi going up to Heaven, so I had the reassurance that I knew I was going to see him again when my time came. I took a huge amount of solace in the embrace of Jesus and the peace of God that I found by talking with Him and reading His Word. I realised, through the poem I was given, "And God Said", and the Bible, that He understood what I was going through and wanted me to find peace and have strength. After all, He lost His Son too!

I am still constantly turning to Him as I face the times ahead, both the hard times and the good times, which I need to enjoy without Levi. It is sometimes very difficult, but I know that I'll be ok.

The Lord will always make something good come from bad. At Levi's funeral, we asked for donations to SIDS Research in lieu of flowers and raised almost $1,000 in Levi's memory.

Through Levi's death and this book, I hope to help you navigate this difficult time, and perhaps it can also teach others the value of precious time and their children, encouraging them to spend a little extra quality time with their children.

Finally, I pray for every person reading this book that peace and comfort will be with you, or, if you are the support person, for someone going through this most challenging time of life, that you have the compassion, wisdom, and kindness to pass on that peace and comfort.

Thank you for your support in purchasing this book.

God bless all of you,
Patricia Lyons (nee: Rasker)

"I can do everything through Him who gives me strength."
(Philippians 4:13)

LEVI M RASKER

Levi M Rasker

1/7/98 – 13/9/99

MY LITTLE MUNCHKIN MAN

WE LOVED YOU A LOT
BUT GOD LOVED YOU MORE

REST IN PEACE

www.ingramcontent.com/pod-product-compliance
Lightning Source LLC
Chambersburg PA
CBHW061211070526
44583CB00025B/3200